THE NO NORMAL LEADER

Published by No Normal Publishing

Paperback ISBN-13: 978-1-8384249-0-9
.epub eBook ISBN-13: 978-1-8384249-1-6
.mobi eBook ISBN-13: 978-1-8384249-2-3

Produced in the United Kingdom

Cover and layout design by www.spiffingcovers.com

THE NO NORMAL LEADER

THE LEADERSHIP HABITS NECESSARY TO THRIVE IN A "NO NORMAL" WORLD

WILLIAM ROGERS
JONATHAN BRADLEY
DAVID COULL

INTRODUCTION

Though three men may have started out on this writing journey following a slightly whimsical, somewhat jocular and fanciful conversation about the new realities each was facing in both their private and commercial lives, their banter-fuelled and good-humoured verbal outbidding of each other as to their own 'no normal, new normal' world, led them to reach one, inevitable conclusion: write a book!

And so, it came to be. Friends and business colleagues for the best part of twenty years, Jonathan Bradley, Dave Coull and William Rogers determined that they would bring together, in one place, their thought-provoking ideas, practical and grounded advice, decades of commercial experience and advocacy of cultural rigour. But where to start?

In this book, it's argued that the 'no normal' world in which we live, is the epitome of the 'new normal' and, the necessities which follow from that, require businesses, voluntary organisations and public bodies to rethink, re-assess and re-invent their cultural, organisational and strategic approach to everything they do.

But, as they delve a bit deeper, they argue that the 'no normal' of today has always been. There is no 'new normal'. For all the advocacy of those who claim we have entered a new world of change and re-appraisal, in truth, such a proposition is simply wrong.

In this book, whilst the fundamentals may be re-examined and the failings of some approaches laid bare, they argue that the 'new' is not, in fact, new at all, and it should certainly not be assumed to be so.

The 'new normal' experience that many claim we are now all part of, is merely an extension of what is already the case and always has been. There may be different names and reference points, but new, it is not. 'New normal' has a shelf-life; 'no normal' does not. What *is* 'new' is the need for a faster and more dynamic response – readiness.

Nevertheless, if you can't really be bothered to read the book, you could turn to page 75 and grade your readiness for the 'no normal' world by simply filling in the self-assessment test.

Good luck!

CHAPTER 1

The 'No Normal' World

How many of us would ever have to work again, if every time somebody declared something as 'the new normal,' we were handed a ten-pound note? It's a pandemic. It's a dot.com bubble, which has just burst. It's a banking crisis. Boom and bust have been abolished, except they haven't!

Things will never be the same again. To quote a well-known phrase from The Firm's[1] 1987 song, *Star Trekkin'*: in *Star Trek*, "It's life, Jim, but not as we know it." The clamour of those advancing new 'norms', accompanied by the chorus of those who advocate such propositions as exclusively 'new,' is almost deafening in such circumstances.

And the answer to the question posed in the first paragraph? Quite. By now, we'd have fistfuls of tenners and almost all of us could put our feet up, lay back and enjoy our early retirement.

The 'new normal' argument is, of course, nonsense. We want to lay out in this book, the argument that it is *both* the cultural personality and responsibility of a business, along with the speed of assimilation and response that needs to change. The need for more dynamism, speed and how to generate them with less haste is the true challenge. Everything else, in essence, remains the same.

Yes, it's fair to say that particular circumstances or events are

1. The Firm: British music act, which had hits in the 1980s with novelty songs

'new', but the underlying principles, the strategic and operational challenges which wrap themselves around a business, each and every year, can always be boiled down to the same thing.

The various factors that lead us into the 'no normal' environment are often different and can be 'new'. However, there is nothing about them that cannot be written at the bottom of a long list of "types" of challenges a business faces.

As Peter Drucker[2] once argued, "The greatest danger in times of turbulence is not the turbulence – it is to act with yesterday's logic."

Bluntly, and in our view, crucially, it is: 1) the attitude, 2) behaviour and 3) practice within a business that matters most. With those three things to the fore, the capability and readiness, with which an organisation responds to circumstances confronting it, is at its maximum state.

History is littered with the commercial corpses of those companies that failed to respond to the circumstances that presented before them. There is a litany of missed opportunities and management 'blind spots', all well documented. No doubt many could rattle off such a list. The nature of such stories and examples, however grand and extraordinary, may well point to what some consider to be failings of judgement or complacency of thinking. But, in truth, it's hard to work through any of these examples without coming to the conclusion that, in reality, it was a combination of a lack of correct attitude, behaviour and practice that made the damage. It was almost certainly the culture or the personality of each of these businesses, which failed them.

It is our belief that, whatever specific circumstances might confront a business, whilst acknowledging that each of those might be a new problem, it is the company's capability of

2. Peter Ferdinand Drucker, 1909–2005: Management consultant, educator and author

managing such circumstances that matters. Is its personality designed to respond in the right way?

How does the management team think, adapt and act? The 'new normal' is limiting and restrictive. It represents a series of particularly specific and perhaps personal issues, each of which cannot be foreseen or anticipated. But these are only recognised at the time they become evident, but they are not sufficiently powerful to represent a 'new normal' in business terms. They are, each and every one – pandemic- or credit crisis-related –issues that will naturally emerge and in response to which businesses need to adapt.

Too often, such 'new' specifics are translated into reasons why this didn't happen, or that couldn't happen. This then opens the way to what we define as 'excuse-thinking' ('excuse-think' for short).

'Excuse-think' is the first line of defence for poorly managed businesses. It's never the management's fault. How could they possibly have seen this coming? What could anyone have done? There's not a business that could have managed this differently. We are suffering the consequences of an unexpected and unanticipated tidal wave of problems. And so it goes on.

In many respects, and to be a touch academic for a moment, this situation is similar to the classic 'man the defences' reaction that appears almost immediately when a problem has reared its ugly head. There is a tendency towards 'excuse-think' without thinking with clarity on the situation. More haste, less speed required. Without this attitude, the problem can evolve into something created to conveniently manage the company's insecurities or shortcomings. This becomes the core of their inadequate response.

This latter type of reaction moves through three primary approaches, sometimes all at the same time! We will outline them here:

1) The attempt to rationalise things can result in a change to the explanation of what has actually occurred. Of course, if it weren't what it actually was, it would be a different scenario.

2) Or it might be the use of an intellectual assessment, which seeks to create an almost academic review of the circumstances. It might be a pressing matter but let's address it as an intellectual exercise only.

3) And, finally, the projection of the problem on to something or someone else, as in 'passing the buck'. It has to be them, or that, carrying the responsibility for our present predicament.

Any, or all of these reactions contribute enormously and even amplify the 'excuse-think' problem.

Now, of course, certain things can emerge which will kill off any business but, by and large, most 'new' challenges can be managed and the majority seen off. It is the readiness of the management team and the cultural environment in which the organisation operates that will matter more than anything else when the storm clouds gather overhead.

We believe that if you are the manager or leader of a business and you consider yourself to have normal attitudes, normal behaviours and normal practices, there's a danger that you might waste your time reading this book. But, for those of you that are not (or those of you who have decided you don't want to be), we'd ask that you open your eyes and your ears to the challenges we want to confront you with as you make your way, chapter by chapter, into our 'no normal' world.

We want to take you on a journey through an almost Darwinian adventure as we attempt to persuade you that the inception and gestation, of this 'no normal' proposition, stems from sound logic, robust enquiry and commercial necessity.

We advocate the 'no normal' proposition because it readies

an organisation to deal with the effects of the catastrophic, the evolutionary, the revolutionary as well as the continuous and discontinuous.

In short, 'no normal' is the underlying premise that business leaders should apply to *all* their business thinking and planning because it is these disconcerting, unnerving and potentially destructive factors that are, and will always be, the norm. They are not 'new', but they do present themselves as such if you allow them to do so.

'No normal' is a belief built on a realisation that a different type of strategy is required and that that is, in itself, built upon a need for radical and cultural change. It is a response to a growing state of inertia taking root in organisations, large and small.

Future success and prosperity for many businesses is now dependent upon urgent cultural transformation.

We all face uncertainty and doubt, but it is so often the cultural order in which they are placed that determines whether we approach them with a sense of arrogance, or necessary care and consideration.

There will no doubt be many other quotes to pick from, but as early as the seventeenth century, we can find thoughtful references to the 'certainty vs doubt' consideration. Francis Bacon[3] wrote in *The Advancement and Proficience of Learning Divine and Human*, 'If a man will begin with certainties, he shall end in doubts, but if he will be content to begin with doubts, he shall end in certainties'.

In a world of uncertainties, the 'no normal' locks in readiness, prepares for innovation through the examination of doubts and options and enhances the capability of an organisation to cope.

---

3. Francis Bacon, 1561–1626: English philosopher and statesman

Within the pages of this book, we share some thoughts, tips, tricks and tools that should help you navigate your way through what some regard and argue as 'new', but that we maintain and will argue, is no such thing.

CHAPTER 2

What is 'Normal' and Why do we Crave it?

The word 'normal' comes from the Latin word '*normalis*', which originally described something regulated by a carpenter's square. Something built this way would be ""normed"" to have angles that were perfectly aligned to fit a general pattern. The word eventually gave us the broader sense that something normal fitted a standard pattern, or which might be considered the average.

The word 'normality' today (or 'normalcy' in the US), is deemed to be something that implies conformity or behaviour consistent with either an individual or organisation. Commonly, normality is often perceived to be good, as opposed to abnormality, which is all too often perceived to be bad or has a stigma attached to it.

There is an argument that also implies normal as being the average or median of a set of data. Norms are standards by which behaviours are measured, for good or ill. Statistically, normal behaviours also establish themselves as social norms. What was once unacceptable can precisely become the opposite.

Human beings like going back to 'normal'. They seem to have an emotional attachment to it, which overrides many other factors. It is often the reason too many people dislike and even fear, change. Moving away from something that has been representative of their life or representative of their very being, is disconcerting and often, felt to be abnormal.

The word 'normal' is a much more powerful word than might, at first, be considered. The philosopher, Charles E Scott,[4] suggests that the word 'normal' possesses a level of "power to divide and distinguish things" and, before we know it, sneakily manages to remove our thinking from description to prescription!

To take just one issue – sexuality. We begin with what is one incontrovertible fact: the majority of people in the world are heterosexual. From that one observable fact, we then construct a hierarchy based upon that 'reality', establishing that heterosexuality is the 'norm'.'

Thus, the fact with which we started our process has, perfectly understandably, become the standard or the 'norm'. Everything that diverges from such a standard is not merely different but becomes abnormal and, therefore, worse than normal. Though this position may be unintended at the outset, if unchecked and not argued with, it is often from such assessments of normality that prejudice all too frequently, grows and flourishes. 'Normal' then becomes introducible, even the unconscious and unanticipated advocate of division and conflict; hardly the 'normal' state in which most people wish to live their lives.

The sociologist, Allan Horwitz,[5] argues that those who wish to identify 'normality' usually turn to three different definitions. Let's discuss them here:

1) Statistical. The 'normal' is whatever trait most people in a group display. In other words, 'normal' is whatever is typical and what most people do. The danger of accepting this as the basis upon which 'normality' is established and then accepted is that it can bestow upon the most abnormal of behaviours, a level of normality that other, different groups, would find repugnant. Was the 'norm' of racism and genocide

4. Charles E Scott, American philosopher and distinguished professor of philosophy
5. Allan Horwitz, American sociologist

perpetrated by those in Nazi Germany in the 30s and 40s a 'normal' philosophy for humans to hold? Our view, clearly, is that it was not. It was a 'new normal' in Nazi Germany, but it was not 'normal' for our society.'

2) 'Normal' might be assessed as some form of 'ideal' state and, very much as an aspirational objective. Normal-as-ideal might be in harmony with normal-as-ubiquitous, but it may well be very different. To continue with our example of Germany in the 30s and 40s, Nazism might well have been widespread at that time, but by any civilised standard, it was not 'normal' because it totally failed to live up to the ideal society most of us wish to see and live in. We would argue that most people want a degree of compassion to rest at the heart of the society in which they live and the Germany of the 30s and 40s failed every test relating to that aspiration.

3) Biological function. Horwitz looks to evolutionary science and defines normality "in terms of how humans are biologically designed by natural selection to function." What is normal behaviour for a human being, which makes it fit to thrive? The capacity to feel shame when betraying a loved one? The desire for one's offspring to survive?

All three of these definitions, statistical, normal and biological, as well as aspirational and functional, sometimes end up bumping against each other and all have their place in an assessment of what the norm might be.

Our belief is that whatever the 'new' component part of any particular crisis might be, it is the specific challenge that confronts us, not the fact that there *is* a challenge that is, of itself, normal. It is how we adapt and react as a result of our attitude, practice and behaviour that determine whether we manage, respond and survive.

And for that to apply, we need to keep it real and ready our organisation for the 'no normal' world. Readiness cannot always be found in growth or forward-thinking momentum either. It will sometimes demand that the consequences of the 'no normal' approach will require us to do things we hadn't expected to do.

To quote an American five-star general of the army, General Douglas MacArthur,[6] "We are not retreating. We are advancing in another direction." It is in the haste and readiness; the preparedness to take such decisions, that success ultimately lies. And for that to apply, the organisation itself needs to be prepped and ready.

In Dr Carole Dweck's[7] book, *Mindset*, she argues that, 'Mindsets frame the running account that's taking place in people's heads. They guide the whole interpretation process. The fixed mindset creates an internal monologue that is focused on judging. The growth mindset is also continuously monitoring what's going on, but their internal monologue is not about judging themselves and others in this way. They're attuned to the implications for learning and constructive action."

In other words, a growth mindset is crucial, accompanied by a fierce willingness to learn.

The 'no normal' world requires just such a mindset.

---

6. General Douglas MacArthur, 1880–1964: American five-star general and Field Marshal of the Philippine Army
7. Dr Carole Dweck, American psychologist

CHAPTER 3

The 'No Normal' Necessity

'No normal' is reality.

The false premise that is 'new normal" is established as a result of the desire to explain and create 'new' norms, which then represent 'excuse-think", which all too many business leaders leverage to narrate what conveniently appears to be yet another unidentified and completely 'new' commercial state.

We describe the 'no normal' proposition as necessary because we believe that it is.

The 'no normal' approach, if comprehensively applied, is a force for good. It represents the dynamic responsiveness that aligns neatly and smartly with enlightened self-interest.

In today's ever-changing climate, we need to learn, unlearn and relearn as we fly towards our moving target, building our plane in mid-air as we go.

To move your thinking into the space we are trying to open up, just ask yourself a few well-chosen and directed questions:

1) How old is new? The 'new normal' is only new for a relatively short period of time.

2) When the internet began to infiltrate every nook and cranny of personal and business life, did it represent a 'new' challenge to business and organisational activity? Of course it did. In fact, in many respects, it revolutionised the way

many businesses operated.

3) But how long did it take before that 'new normal' became, well, 'normal'?'

The particular and specific impact that the internet had on trading, researching and communicating, was revolutionary. But the challenge it represented to businesses was entirely in line with the evolutionary process of new ways of acting that have materialised throughout the ages. What was different was not the fact that the internet presented itself as a change or, indeed, represented a 'new normal,' but that it merely represented yet the latest in a long line of challenges to confront commercial activity across the world.

Those businesses that had the kind of 'personality and cultural approach' which made them ready to adapt; 'they opened up their practices and behaviours to this 'new kid on the block' and prospered. They developed an internally honed response to the fresh-faced challenger that this new invention represented. Indeed, some of the most powerful and globally influential companies around today did not even exist prior to the internet's invention.

The final question at this point is:

4) Why do you think that putting everything back to normal will solve everything? It's quite likely you'd like to do this, but you won't be sure whether or not it is possible. One thing is accepting that the changes a pandemic brings are new. Accepting that those same identifiable and particular events will, in some way, herald in a completely 'new normal' is, we contend, simply 'excuse-think.'

What should be 'normal' in your organisation is not the acceptance that it has to swing around in the breeze every time something new and specific arrives on the scene, but that your operation is primed and geared up to face any challenge it confronts, precisely because it is considered as normal to do so.

It is normal that challenges arise, normal that, from time to time, your business or organisation will be under threat. It's normal that the strategy followed for years may start to unravel, just like it's normal that new technology may force a wholesale review of operational management and process. It's also normal that what your business has represented for years may need to be completely re-appraised in light of new information and threat.

'No normal' is normal.

How come you think you are in control? As managers and leaders, we all fall into this trap! We are certainly in control of those things we can influence and internally direct. But in all respects, to imply or even advocate that we are running the entire show is both arrogant and foolhardy.

Might it be that this is one of the main reasons why so many business leaders are too slow to react to the challenges that confront them?

There is not a single leader of a single company anywhere in the world who is 'in control'.

Sure, if they are any good, they'll have a set of strategic objectives and clearly defined goals and they'll be focused on productivity improvements and efficiency gains. With any luck, they'll realise just how important their company culture is and be providing some support and internal initiatives to enhance it still further.

But, apart from those specifically internal elements, when it comes to unpredictable challenges and the unknown, what leaders/managers are in control of is how well they equip their organisation with the cultural and procedural tools to be ready – ready for the unpredictable, ready for the latest 'new' particular challenge, ready for the chaos of unexpected change and all those extraordinary evolutionary steps that lie in front of us.

'No normal' is about the underlying state of readiness that your organisation already has in place so that it can respond to whatever situation it finds itself in.

At the risk of boring you, it's about the personality of the organisation. It's about its capability and readiness and, if you remember from earlier, that comes from its attitude, behaviour and practices. If it's culturally robust and dynamic enough, it'll cope, unless it's simply impossible to do so. And if that latter point proves to be so, there's nothing you could have done in any event!

To fail, to risk, to transition and to try. All are elements of dynamism and readiness.

As one of the greatest leaders of the 20th century, Winston Churchill,put it, "Success is going from failure to failure without a loss of enthusiasm." In some respects, such an approach might seem unproductive. How many failures should one organisation accept? But the context for such failure is crucial and if that context is to innovate, to challenge with good intent and to maximise the input of others, the impact upon the readiness of an organisation to face challenge can be profound.

Do you think you can predict the future? Okay, so your middle name might be Nostradamus, but for most of us we are mere mortals and the answer to that is no. Let's suppose you might even be one of those miracle workers who did, indeed, make a prediction that came off. Why do you think that? Perhaps because you've done it before, you'll be able to do it again?

This is best described by a certain famous Queen[8] song: 'Is this the real life? Is this just fantasy?' The real fantasy of believing in one's own ability to foretell the future is, indeed, about as far away from real commercial life as it's possible to get.

The 'no normal' approach facilitates continuous review and drives change of itself, licensing your teams to challenge and encourage adaptation and creativity. It's a leveller and it recognises bravery, tolerates considered failure, strengthens the role of the imaginers and innovators and drives performance capability. So too, it focuses on outcomes and facilitates the management of different futures.

The dynamism with which a company acts, and the effectiveness with which it thinks, can only be maximised if its personality is constructed around the very potential challenges that it would prefer not to confront.

If we take a trip down memory lane for just a moment, the commercial world is littered with the corpses of companies that failed to recognise the value of new ideas that appeared to challenge their very being, but which would have been their saviour.

Kodak employee, Steven Sassoon,[9] actually invented the first self-contained digital camera in 1975. Describing his experience at the time, "But it was filmless photography, so (the) management's reaction was 'that's cute – but don't tell anyone about it'," he said. The leaders of Kodak failed to see digital photography as a disruptive technology, and the rest is history.

8. Sir Winston Leonard Spencer Churchill, 1874–1965: British statesman, orator and author who, as prime minister (1940–1945, 1951–1955), rallied the British people during World War II and led his country from the brink of defeat to victory Queen song – Bohemian Rhapsody. Album: A Night at the Opera (1975)

9. Steven J Sassoon, American electrical engineer and inventor

And so, yet again, attitude, behaviour and practice equal capability. **Be ready.**

CHAPTER 4

'No Normal' Readiness

In chapter 6 we discuss 'The Octopus of the No Normal Approach'. We even tell you why we call it the octopus. But ahead of that, we want to take you through what we mean by 'no normal' readiness and why it is so fundamentally important to this approach.

One of the difficult assessments to make about any organisation is precisely the one part that we agree is the most important, out of all the functions it possesses. What we can all do is focus on those things that are most likely to get our organisation into a position where it will be at its most ready, whatever that ends up being.

Though we will look at some specific aspects and influences a little later on, ultimately it's the generality of human relationships that will create the state of perpetual readiness. This should ensure that dynamism is a prolific influencer of how a business operates.

Jean-Paul Sartre[10] suggested that confrontation was the basis for all authentic human relationships and, whilst we are not arguing that daily life in every business should start with hassle and angst, we do believe that real trusting and respectful relationships stem from the openness of discussion and debate.

---

10. Jean-Paul Charles Aymard Sartre, 21 June 1905 – 15 April 1980: French philosopher, playwright, novelist, screenwriter, political activist, biographer and literary critic

Therefore, tension and 'well-managed conflict' must, from time to time, challenge the status quo and the 'We've always done it like that' mentality.

To be ready, it will be necessary for the comfortable balance between a chosen direction and the means to get there, to be disturbed on a fairly regular basis. Without doing so, we are far less likely to be ready for a 'no normal' world in which 'no normal' is the only game in town.

Having got that off our chests, here are some of those specifics to focus on that we mentioned a little earlier.

LEADERSHIP

One of the most critical areas of human input into a state of 'no normal' readiness is that of leadership. Leaders are important – good leaders are critical. Without focused, clear and engaging leadership, very little is truly committed to or effectively embedded in an organisation.

The leader counts. Whether man or woman, without the all-embracing advocacy and practical engagement of the leadership of a business, things simply won't get nailed. By all-embracing, we mean all-embracing. Simply shoving a few slogans on a wall, buying a print of a sailing ship as a visual embodiment of the 'team' or making the odd speech about how important everyone is, won't cut it.

Leaders can't simply 'talk the talk', they have to 'walk the walk' and walk it well!

The leader of any organisation is the flag bearer, the epitome of the cultural style he or she wishes to adopt. Reflective of its values and approach, if the leader fails to 'be' the company and all it seeks to do and 'be', it's quite likely to be curtains for the rest.

Leaders need to be ready – they need to consider intuitively and act decisively. They need to lead the way by opening their organisation to challenge and constructive criticism from those around them and they need to show contentment in doing so. Gearing up an organisation to develop a 'no normal' approach needs consistent and committed leadership. Without it, don't bother starting.

Those that have authority in a business, particularly the individuals that have people- management responsibilities, are often those that have the day-to-day task of delivery. In departments after section, after team, after group, managers are often task-focused and charged with producing something or even everything. Theirs is the world of objectives and results.

Their roles will often include an element of leadership and coaching, as well as all those management functions which almost always absorb too much of their time, including the form-filling for three- or six-monthly appraisals and time spent mentoring.

These leaders are often the real glue of an organisation. They hold things together, manage the latest personnel crisis, or reflect on the need for developing new ways to boost productivity levels.

Their understanding across a whole range of subjects is almost always better than that of their own bosses but they are also, too often, held hostage by their own responsibilities. They often have little time or, sadly, inclination to contribute to the wider policy and operation debate.

Managers need to be readied for a 'no normal' future. They need to have their boundaries reviewed, the cage bars removed and their contributions regularly listened to with appreciation.

Many business leaders claim to believe that their teams or the individual people who comprise them are the most important asset a business has. It's a view we subscribe to but one we also accept is open to 'excuse-think' and abuse.

One of the saddest features of too much management culture is that the lower-grade workers are often the first to suffer when commercial reality hits home. The 'selfish and greedy' characteristics of certain leaders and managers emerge, unchecked, at times of crisis.

We only have to look at the appalling attitude of many senior executives and business owners at the very top of businesses to feel disappointed and depressed at the wholesale disregard for those who toil at the other end of the business' influential curve. This leads to fat pay cheques, big bonuses and a selfish obsession with making money at others' expense. Sometimes, the bigger the company, the hungrier its leadership appears.

Here are our top three representative culprits, redacted, of course, because we don't want to be sued. You can mentally insert your top three here instead:

■■■

■■■

■■■

One thing we earnestly hoped would emerge from the wreckage that COVID-19 brought, for example, is a re-appraisal of the roles that some of the lowest paid in society have and how we reflect their contribution to our country and community. Who would have classified supermarket workers as 'essential' prior to the pandemic? Or the care-home worker, managing on the minimum wage and often struggling to make ends meet?

In business, just as in the general wider society, it is the teams who toil away delivering a product who need to be engaged and encouraged in maximising their contributions to gain appreciation for their efforts. By open conversations, engaging communications, listening, responding and the too often unused words, cared for, or valued, if you prefer – it is these groups from which innovation, problem solving and new ideas are most likely to emerge. Very few people turn up to work in the morning with a plan to cause damage or disrupt the business they work for. They should always be treated in that way and on that basis.

Culturally, authoritative and egocentric business owners do the very cause of capitalism a grave disservice and need to reflect upon their responsibilities as well as the size of their bank balances. Too many managers and leaders 'transmit but do not receive' and they are becoming liabilities to the very businesses they are trying to lead.

Businesses which really want to be ready for the 'no normal' need every personnel component of their organisation becoming 'no normal-ready' and that includes their most important asset – their people.

It's hard to think of a business or a sector, which, from time to time, doesn't have a problem with systems or procedures.

The critical approach to adopt for procedural and system readiness for the 'no normal' world is, along with flexibility, a willingness to review. The more rigid any of these necessary elements of business operation is, the less able to adapt and innovate a business and, as a consequence, the more frustrated your people will become.

'Computer says no' is just about the most frustrating set of words a human being can hear in a work environment.

Future-proofing your operation by ensuring the scalability, flexibility and overall innovative capability of procedures and systems, should not be underestimated. Will this approach require the allocation of time and money? Yes, of course it will. To think that the creation of a truly dynamic and 'culturally ready' business can be prepared without either is delusional. Is it worth it? Of course it is!

'No normal' thinking across each and every one of these key areas, as opposed to the usual 'back to normal' or even 'new normal' thinking, will be key to developing the kind of dynamic operation that can respond to any manageable challenge with speed, flexibility and full engagement. You should now understand why 'no normal' readiness and good leadership is so fundamentally important to this approach.

In short: attitude + behaviour + practice = readiness

CHAPTER 5

The Power of the 'No Normal' Approach

COMPETITIVE ADVANTAGE

Of course, it's what every business seeks. Truthfully though, very few have a product or market dominance that overrides most other factors. Most businesses compete with others for their share of the market.

Thus, the competitive advantage they prise from everything they do, matters. But it's not just 'a new product' or 'a better marketing campaign' that drives such an advantage on a permanent basis. It's the capability of the enterprise itself to adapt and respond to market conditions and the effectiveness of those who deliver, which embeds such advantage.

Short-term thinking inevitably produces short-term results, but some are positive, of course. For most businesses though, short-termism merely papers over the cracks of the inadequacy of strategic thinking and management execution.

Building an organisation that lives and breathes enhanced capability will, ultimately, drive competitive position and, in our view, advantage as a result.

Imagine, for just a moment, how different commercial life would be for a business if every time it was confronted with a manageable but serious crisis, it simply moved into 'readiness mode'. The behaviour of its individuals and teams was such that they were already geared up and anticipating the challenges ahead. There was concern, possibly anxiety (but no fear) and certainly no dread.

The practices that were already in place ensured the smooth operation of the enterprises' facilitated faster responses – and they were even more adaptive to necessity as a result.

Imagine if all these were hard-wired into the very essence, culture and personality of the operation.

EFFECTIVE DECISION-MAKING

We all know that the wider the experience of the leadership and management team of any business, the more likely it is that decisions will be made in a more effective, considered and measured way. Or they should be!

If we are honest with ourselves, as leaders and managers, we also know that none of us has a monopoly of wisdom and that, regrettably, we've also all made our fair share of mistakes. That's as true today as it always has been and always will be, BUT we can make fewer mistakes and learn from them. No leader is an island of perfection. We only have to look at some of the horror stories briefly referenced earlier in the pages of this book, to realise that!

Surely, it's better to have the alternative opinion, the innovative idea, the creative thought-making and even the contrary individual, openly and eagerly contributing to decision-making and the consideration of different sets of circumstances, when the wave hits?

So, our approach to 'effective decision-making' is not one which proposes that decisions are merely taken effectively, but one which challenges the essence of the word 'effective' in such circumstances.

The more staff who are given the opportunity to speak up about possible sensible solutions or ideas, the wider the facilitation of any matter requiring consideration. Some companies choose to do this through a questionnaire, as often people are more likely to speak their views on all subjects more freely, rather than face to face.

Obviously, this cannot be about every person in an organisation taking corporate decisions that require a degree of confidentiality prior to them being actioned. But, what it *does* mean is that when considering those very strategic and operational matters that *should* and *do* require the greatest application of brainpower and review, it's the structure that many levels of the business should have input or influence on that is likely to be the most effective way of arriving at the best conclusion. Why? Because the default position within the organisation automatically wires that approach in.

The more your managers and teams are 'inclusively engaged' on a day-to-day, year-on-year basis, the more ready they will be to contribute constructively and innovatively when a real crisis hits.

ENHANCED COMMUNICATION

Let's begin by considering exactly what this means. We all know what we think communication is and that 'enhanced' means it's a step up from communication in a normal and traditional way. That, we accept, is reality.

However, this area represents one of the most difficult aspects of running a business, as well as one of the most constant failures, which almost any sized organisation, acknowledges it has:

- Send an e-mail ✓
- Send an internal memo ✓
- Have a team meeting ✓
- Stick a note up on the noticeboard ✓
- Call a meeting ✓

All of these represent just a few examples of frequently utilised forms of internal communication. They are all, of course, perfectly legitimate. We have all used them and will probably continue to do so.

However, what we mean by 'enhanced communication' is the DEPTH of such activity, not merely the surface act that delivers it.

The regularity is important, if not essential, but so too is the degree to which communications are meaningful and challenging.

We believe sharing information and asking questions is the key to unlocking a level of two-way communication within an organisation that will ultimately deliver a depth of communication unrivalled in your competitors. The key is also in following up. If you have made a call or sent an e-mail, don't just tick it off the list and leave it there. Seek to gain an answer if you have not received a response within a given time.

Trust stems from a combination of words and deeds. To start to build that trust, you must first expose yourself and the organisation to precisely the kind of internal scrutiny and communicative depth that most leaders and managers fear.

Do not fear it. Trust your teams and they will trust you right back and communicate in a way which will open up a veritable rainbow of ideas and engagement. At the end of this will come that little pot of gold, in the form of an idea or suggestion that might otherwise never have seen the light of day.

Essential to that generation of ideas and willingness by others to openly contribute, is a ready listening ear and the passing on of due credit. Saying 'thank you' often and sincerely is a great way of encouraging ideas and highlighting the appreciation that should always accompany them. Plus, it doesn't cost anything!

Enhanced communication is a two-way process, not one. Go deep and go meaningful. Anything else is 'excuse-think'. And if you are not totally committed to the process in its most rounded of senses, don't start. Don't even go there! Embracing the good, the bad and sometimes even the ugly may not always be a pleasant experience for any leader, but it's essential.

Do not give your team a voice if you end up being the first one to stop listening to it.

IMPROVED PRODUCTIVITY AND EFFICIENCY

We don't know a business anywhere in the world that does not want to see an improvement in both productivity and efficiency. And why not? It's fundamentally important to secure competitive advantage and commercial success.

As stated earlier, if the cultural environment, personality and all the other elements of your business are in place, these two things will inevitably follow. Why?

Quite simply because the level of engagement will rise, ideas will flow (often from the bottom up) and the desire to go further and faster by almost everyone in your organisation, will generate that very result.

In your organisation, it's highly likely that unless it is already a 'no normal' type of operation, there are people sitting on ideas that would improve things somewhere, but are not feeding them in because they are either too frightened to do so, don't have the confidence to express themselves, or, they don't believe it is their place. Again, this is where the six-monthly appraisal comes in, or the questionnaire opportunity.

Whichever one of these (or even all of them) might apply, just think for a moment: what is this delay in conversation or input costing the business? Do the maths. Let's assume that whatever the thought or idea is, it makes just a 1% difference to revenues or even operating profitability, year-on-year. And then, let's assume you had two such ideas (out of the hundred you got every year) which were enacted. Do the maths again!

Lifting the lid on the pent-up innovation and creativity that lurks beneath it does nothing but good. Allowing ideas to flow, criticisms to be made and innovation to flourish, as well as welcoming a little risk and even more failure, in the long run, is transformational.

Trust your people and give them the freedom to engage without the threat of retribution. In return they'll add value, efficiency and productivity to the company because they'll appreciate they can contribute to the company in more ways than one.

CULTURAL DYNAMISM AND ENGAGEMENT

What do you want the personality of your business to have? If you don't want it to be dynamic and engaging, we'd ask you why you're bothering to even think about it!

Confronting the new specific challenges which emerge with regularity during the lifespan of a business is all part of the 'no normal' world. We've already listed all too many of them earlier in the pages of this book. Some may be new to us, but they can all be added to a list that generally includes, as referenced earlier, the catastrophic, evolutionary, revolutionary, continuous and discontinuous factors.

The organisation that looks at each of these particular factors, through anything other than a 'no normal' lens, is an organisation that will never be ready or prepared.

Why? Because whatever the challenge, if it is always perceived to be new and strategically so, then it becomes accepted thinking that new solutions are also necessary and, thus, a new way of working through them needs to be found.

But if your organisation was, of itself, already in that 'head space' and simply looked at any new specific challenge as one of a number of different issues that needed to be tackled and responded to quickly in the normal way that your business usually responds, then you're already a long way down the road to resolving the issue, if it is resolvable.

COVID-19 was a challenging set of circumstances and will continue to be for quite some time. It is a 'new' virus and the implications of its impact are considerable. However, is it really something that cannot be categorised as one more, albeit different, challenge that a business faces?

Taking a closer look at COVID-19, a business leader could not influence testing policy, intensive-care capacity and public policy in terms of social distancing and personal separation, business-support measures or the immediate and long-term economic consequences of each of these policies enacted. Like the team ready to race their boat down the stretch of water in front of them, the only thing they can do is influence what goes on *in*side their boat, not *out*side of it.

Preparing your business for the threats, challenges and opportunities it will face, whatever they may be, is both a necessary and sensible approach to take.

The level of cultural dynamism and engagement that flows through the veins of your operation will be one of the most critically important factors in establishing how 'ready' your business will be when the time comes, as it will.

Henry Ford[11] was credited as having said, "Obstacles are those frightful things you see when you take your eyes off your goal." Those who argue that we are always faced with a 'new normal', miss the point. 'New normal' is an obstacle to long-term preparation and thinking. Don't take your eyes off the goal. That goal is readiness and that readiness is achieved by capability. Capability is achieved through a 'no normal' approach.

---

11. Henry Ford, 1863–1947: American industrialist and business magnate, founder of the Ford Motor Company

CHAPTER 6

The Octopus of the 'No Normal' Approach

The octopus is a truly remarkable creature. Let's take one example of the almost three hundred species which can be found in the world's oceans – the common octopus.

The common octopus has a unique appearance. It has a massive bulbous head, large eyes, eight distinctive arms and it has three hearts.

It has an extraordinary array of defensive options that can be deployed to avoid or thwart its attackers. Its first line of defence is to hide in plain sight by using the pigments in its skin to almost instantly match the colours and even the textures of its surroundings. By releasing a cloud of black ink, which dulls the predator's sense of smell, it can swim away from danger.

It can swim incredibly fast, jetting forwards by expelling water through their mantles and it can squeeze into the most unlikely of spaces where predators can't follow. Incredibly, it can squeeze through any hole that is no larger than its beak, the only hard part of its entire body.

But, if all else fails, it can also lose an arm to a predator and simply regrow it later with no permanent damage. With beak-like jaws, it can also give a nasty nip and its venomous saliva subdues its prey.

A truly remarkable creature and one that we feel reflects so many of the amazing qualities that fit perfectly into the 'no normal' world we advocate.

The octopus truly represents readiness and capability. It has an attitude that makes it a genuinely formidable opponent, a behaviour that sets it apart from other creatures and assists in ensuring its survival and, in both attack and defence, practices which make it incredibly adept at managing situations and new threats to its future.

This is a 'no normal' creature. Like many species of octopus, whether we condone the female eating the male after mating, is another matter altogether!

With eight arms, or tentacles, the dear old octopus also helps us neatly define our own 'eight arms of the 'no normal' approach'. These eight characteristics are, we believe, essential in order to establish capability and readiness for the 'no normal' world.

In the next eight chapters we shall discuss what each tentacle comprises.

THE EIGHT ATTRIBUTES OF 'NO NORMAL' LEADERS

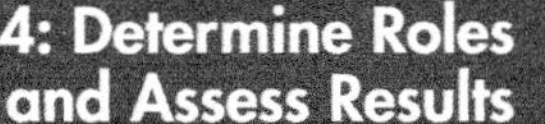

1: Trust

Trusting in other team members and the team as an entity. High trust actions result in high performance results.

2: Entrust

Use a democratic leadership style involving and engaging team members.

3: Challenge and Support

Dealing with conflict openly and transparently using both a challenging and supportive style.

4: Determine Roles and Assess Results

Each team member must understand what they must do (and what they must not do!)

5: Focus on Outcomes

Each goal must have personal meaning and resonance, building commitment and engagement.

6: Make Decisions Wisely

Facilitating dynamic thinking with clear goals, raised awareness, options and wise decision-making.

7: Communicate Openly and Clearly

Communicating with consistency. Bringing words to life with actions.

8: Value Similarity and Difference

Enabling a diversity of viewpoints. Valuing diversity of experience and backgrounds.

CHAPTER 7

Tentacle 1 – Trust

Fundamentally, establishing trust from the top to the bottom of an organisation must be the starting point for any endeavour such as this.

trust *noun: belief or confidence in, or reliance on, the truth, goodness, character, power, ability, etc of someone or something.*

Like most businesses, we suspect you don't have a handy 'trustometer' about, to instantly measure the levels of trust that exist in your business. Somehow, you must be clear in your intent to establish this as the cornerstone of developing your 'no normal' readiness.

Without trust, belief is reduced. Without trust, truth is questioned. Without trust, the perception of reliability falters. Trust comes from the top and can only be delivered by the words, deeds and actions of the leaders and managers of the business.

How did you feel last time someone promised you something and then failed to deliver it?

What did you feel when someone you relied on in a professional capacity, showed disappointing levels of incompetence or a lack of knowledge and ability? Once trust in senior members of the organisation is established, all else flows more readily and considerably more easily.

Establishing trust is, in many ways, similar to being approachable. First, the leaders and managers have, themselves, to do the approaching. You can't magic up trust. It's earned and, without earning it, your task to build a ready-made 'no normal' company just got a lot harder.

Just like your customers, your team won't buy from you until they trust you.

Whilst most good leaders understand all this and reflect the five points in our table above, to a greater or lesser extent, 'no normal' leaders also realise that higher levels of trust also require higher levels of personal obligation and readily accepted responsibility.

As trust is based almost entirely upon the relationships between two human beings, the better you know the person and the more obviously and overtly you value them and their contribution, so too the levels of trust rise and the relationship advances still further. But, this is primarily the responsibility of the person who leads and should not be an expectation placed upon the follower. First and foremost, it is the leader that has to step up in this regard.

If you lack integrity, you're dishonest and you have no sense of genuine, objective fairness, you're pretty much dead in the water anyway when it comes to trust. But, giving practical effect to each of these qualities on a day-to-day basis sharply enhances the value of your personal and professional reputation.

One too often ignored, undervalued and disregarded attribute that all good 'no normal' leaders possess, is consistency. Being the same person every day, acting in the same way every day and delivering 'brand you' every day, whatever the circumstances and wherever you may be, is one of the most beneficial qualities that a great leader possesses.

Predictable and reliable behaviour is fundamentally important to ensure stability and meaningful levels of engagement from those around you. Pleasant one day and then moody the next – what do you think this does, not only to your reputation with your colleagues, but even more importantly, to their confidence in engaging with you?

Which version of you is going to turn up to work each day? This is not a question you want anyone in your team to be asking! It needs to be the same, good version of you turning up, day in and day out.

1: Trust

No normal leaders understand...

- Two-way trust is critically important
- Loyalty to vision and direction is vital
- Trust builds engagement
- Significance of team spirit, belief and participation
- Encouraging, supporting and caring is key to building trust.

Even better when they grasp...

- It is absolutely imperative for delivering on promises
- Trust in a leader relies on a convincing demonstration of competence, knowledge and ability
- Need to show significant regard to relationships, always focused on knowing and valuing people
- Value of acting with total integrity, honesty and fairness
- Need for predictable and reliable behaviour.

CHAPTER 8

Tentacle 2 – Entrust

Leaders come in all shapes and sizes and perform their tasks in different ways. But the essence of the 'no normal' leader is one that oozes the desire for maximising participation right across the organisation that (s)he leads:

- It's a style which recognises that everyone in the organisation has a contribution to make.
- It's a style which comfortably and willingly encourages the delegation of tasks and enhances the levels of autonomy within the business.
- It's a style which values every opinion.
- It's a style which encourages conversation, challenge and open communication, both up and down the hierarchy.
- It's a style which values people as individuals as well as the roles they perform.
- It's a style which communicates in depth, regularly.
- It's a style which is approachable and encouraging.
- It's a style which honestly reflects on mistakes and lessons learned.
- It's a style which encourages calculated risk and necessary failure.

- It's a style built on trust.

It's a style which also has to be, authentically, you and, whilst good leaders will both recognise and understand all of the above attributes, a 'no normal' leader realises that giving practical effect and demonstrating all of these stylistic reference points is equally important.

Practical demonstration is a powerful weapon in the 'no normal' leader's armoury and, without it, opportunities to influence are ignored and moments to establish trust in others, potentially lost.

Being the essence of the cultural environment you wish your business to be is a far more effective and practical way of representing it, than any poster you might decide to put on the walls of your building.

If you are going to both include and empower people within your organisation, you must first create an environment that both respects and values them. Layer on top of that an environment in which they also feel psychologically safe and you will truly achieve a breakthrough in which your team will thrive and your competitors can only envy.

In such an environment, encouraging the calculated risk that all organisations need, managed alongside the toleration of the inevitable failures which follow, creates a dynamic and vibrant culture which will generate formidable levels of engagement right across the enterprise.

The openness and honesty, which both follow from such an approach, accelerate the development of honest feedback and generate a more reflective review of mistakes made and the lessons learned as a consequence.

Everyone knows who the boss is. Everyone knows who his or

her direct line manager is. Very few people fail to understand that, ultimately, someone has to lead, someone has to make an informed decision and someone else has to follow once the direction of travel is determined.

Delivering an authentic 'you' within a cultural environment that oozes inclusion, engagement and trust, removes the sharper, unnecessary edges that the traditional business structures of hierarchy impose.

Getting to such a destination can be a difficult road to travel. But, arriving there makes the journey entirely worth the effort.

2: Entrust

No normal leaders understand...

- Advantage of maximising participation across the organisation
- Everyone in the organisation has a contribution to make – give them their heads
- It's about power with, not over employees. Giving people freedom, empowerment and confidence to make decisions creates greater capability
- Leadership is collective
- Value of encouraging conversation, challenge and open communication.

Even better when they grasp...

- Need to demonstrate self-awareness, awareness of others and what's actually going on
- Developmental benefit of honest feedback, reflecting on mistakes and lessons learned
- Encourage calculated risk and necessary failure
- For people to feel empowered and included they must feel respected, valued and psychologically safe
- Need to remove hierarchy wherever possible.

CHAPTER 9

Tentacle 3 – Challenge and Support

Whilst the first two tentacles of our octopus are clearly focused upon the two essential foundation components that 'no normal' leadership requires, the truly positive and engaging organisations are also those that readily encourage and facilitate both challenge and support.

Both of these elements are two-way – up and down.

The additional rigour that is introduced to a company that facilitates open, but considered and thoughtful challenge of its managers, is extraordinary. And it's not easy for many managers to adapt to this new reality.

The upward challenge is obviously attractive from the perspective of those below. But what this also facilitates is the easier and more effective challenge downwards too.

If the natural, cultural state of the company is for open, upward challenge – considered, thoughtful and always with positive intent – then the manner of the downward challenge soon becomes a powerful and effective process of communication too.

We are not arguing that this has no challenges or, indeed, is not incredibly difficult to achieve at times, particularly for managers and leaders, but what we *do* argue is that the dynamism, openness, engagement and trust that this cultural shift introduces, if sustained, has a remarkable impact.

Support is more than just a pat on the back and a warm smile when things are tough. It's a wraparound, all-encompassing cultural approach within a business that provides 'air-cover' for subordinates if things go wrong on a project or a new idea they've been working on.

It's about allowing risk and failure to be carried out without fear of consequential actions if a go-ahead had been previously given.

It's about creating an environment where the company considers its people as an extension of its family, caring about them when things are tough and wrapping their metaphorical arms around them when needs require it to do so.

It's about those within the organisation, at all levels, looking out for others, particularly when the going gets tough.

Support, like challenge, is an up-and-down proposition and should set just such an objective at the outset.

3: Challenge and Support

No normal leaders understand…

- Need to challenge unsatisfactory performance and behaviour
- People development will maximise potential
- Importance of understanding others to get the best for and from them
- Importance of building rapport and showing empathy
- Need to be clear about benefits and consequences.

Even better when they grasp…

- Focus on building confidence by providing ‘air cover’ for implementing new ideas that carry risk
- Need to ask challenging questions, bring up difficult issues and propose controversial solutions
- Value of communicating in a direct, open and honest manner, even when it’s difficult
- Centring on the desired future outcome helps to clarify what support and challenge may be required
- Merit of being open to challenging feedback and guidance from direct reports.

CHAPTER 10

Tentacle 4 – Determine Roles and Assess Results

This, to some, might be statin' the bleedin' obvious and, of course, it is. But unfortunately and quite often, these two things simply don't happen.

Setting out a clearly defined set of objectives, as well as the responsibilities and authorities that someone has to deliver them, while holding them to account, seems both natural and necessary. Indeed, in the theoretical world of a round table and academic discussion, the entire room of business managers and leaders would agree that this was necessary.

Nonetheless, it does not always happen. We'd actually go as far to say that in the majority of cases, it *doesn't* happen.

Defining someone's role is not always the easiest of things to do effectively. It will often take more time than is afforded to it and, sometimes, the implications of small changes made to someone's role can be ignored in terms of their consequences upon the roles of others.

However, in the main, this is the easier of the two elements. It's the holding to account that is often done inadequately or, in many cases, not at all!

An open, engaging and dynamic cultural environment is not an excuse to permit consequential unaccountability to develop – quite the reverse.

The more engaged people are and the more they are permitted to influence and directly impact policies, procedures and productivity, the more they will all expect everyone, particularly managers and leaders, to accept their responsibilities and deliver on the objectives set.

Holding people to account is not about throwing assorted toys out of the pram and behaving like a five-year-old who has been denied their favourite packet of sweets. In most circumstances, once a manager loses his or her temper it's game over for the relationship. In principle, it's also poor management.

Holding someone to account is entirely appropriate in a business context and yet all too frequently, managers will not confront these issues early enough and, as a consequence, try and work with the individual to improve performance and delivery too late and for too long a time frame. Unfortunately, on occasion, it necessitates the removal of a person much earlier from the organisation. Sometimes it really is as straightforward as that.

It's amazing the number of times someone who was not doing their job well enough or, alternatively, taking the proverbial, has been removed from an organisation and the rest of the team is surprised it took so long for management to act. The team knows when someone isn't fulfilling their role sufficiently and is repeatedly failing to deliver. Teams often fail to comprehend why it takes so long for management to sort it out.

There's no point in someone having a role if they are not expected to be accountable for delivering what they are asked!

The 'no normal' leader expects potential recruits to be considered for their cultural impact as well as their skill set. The better the individual 'fits' within the company culture as well as the rest of their colleagues, the better it will be for all concerned. Simple.

Once recruited, the 'no normal' company environment celebrates, not only the successes of task and effort, but also habitual improvement and cultural shift. Leadership within the 'no normal' state is attuned to and focused upon ensuring that people have a sense of the contribution they make to the organisation and the value that is placed upon it.

As time goes on, a 'no normal' business regularly reviews the levels of enthusiasm and engagement a person has for any given role, as well as the success being made, just as secondary-school children are assessed on their behaviour and attitude to learning. How people 'feel' about their job can be one of the most powerful drivers of the success they ultimately bring to it.

4: Determine Roles and Assess Results

No normal leaders understand...

- Need for clarifying task significance
- Importance of clear model definition, purpose and understanding
- Clear role definition reduces time wasting, unnecessary tension and stress
- Need to ensure skill levels match up to the requirements of the role
- Importance of measuring performance gaps through regular review conversations.

Even better when they grasp…

- Designing and specifying roles that fit operationally and culturally and within a team environment are more likely to succeed
- Value of celebrating effort and habit change as well as results
- Failure can be a necessary step to success
- Helping people feel their job makes a real difference, builds engagement and focus
- Checking sense of responsibility and enthusiasm for the role and its wider impact reduces risk of mission creep.

CHAPTER 11

Tentacle 5 – Focus on Outcomes

It's useful to have a mechanism for both assessing the roles allocated, as well as the process of managing accountability. Any well-led business recognises the need for managing performance as well as establishing clear expectations from the outset.

How this is delivered in any business is a matter of individual preference. Some will search for the simplest process and others a more complex, sophisticated option.

SMART[12] goals is one of the simplest ways of doing this. We've looked at all sorts of potential ideas, models and suggestions and we've ended up back with the most straightforward and well-known one. Sometimes, it's the familiar, well-referenced and most readily understood model or idea that works the best.

That said, it is less important which model is used and much more important that your approach is outcome-led. The focus on outcomes, far more so than the task itself, is key.

In the 'no normal' environment, it'll be important to get your

12. SMART is an acronym that is used to set goals. To make sure your goals are clear and reachable, each one should be:

- Specific (simple, sensible, significant)
- Measurable (meaningful, motivating)
- Achievable (agreed, attainable)
- Relevant (reasonable, realistic and resourced, results-based)
- Time bound (time-based, time limited, time/cost limited)

teams to imagine many different outcomes – something not at all normal in most organisations.

Collective brainstorming may well be a feature of such an approach and leading your team through those desirable and undesirable experiences, should be a necessary componential part of your regular approach to readiness planning. These are often part of team-building days.

'No normal' leaders will recognise that, in addition to their desired outcome delivery, they will also ensure that the ways such outcomes are achieved are also considered carefully.

A facilitative style, often generating the most inclusive and widest level of engagement and team flexibility will often generate more activity and innovative thinking than that of the micro-manager – (s)he will be obsessed with second guessing every element of any given process and controlling each and every outcome.

In summary, the 'no normal' leader is clear but inclusive, timeline focused, flexible where appropriate, facilitative in style, but demanding of result.

5: Focus on Outcomes

No normal leaders understand…

- Importance of performance management, meetings and clarity of outcome required
- Clear expectations on what steps need to be achieved
- Outcome needs to be quantifiable
- Team clear about how everyone involved participates
- A clear process and timescale are essential.

Even better when they grasp…

- Need to kick out micro-management tendencies
- Leaders of outcome-focused meetings use a facilitative style
- Need to give teams flexibility in getting results
- Definition of the outcome decided by the team
- Brainstorming of several options a habitual part of the process.

CHAPTER 12

Tentacle 6 – Make Decisions Wisely

In part, we've referred to this a little earlier in the book.

Under this heading, we wanted to broaden the thinking behind this approach.

It would be hard to imagine anyone disagreeing with the notion that decisions made and based upon careful thought and good judgement are likely to lead to anything other than a wiser choice. Like every other decision, it doesn't mean it'll always be right, but it's more likely to be.

It should go without saying that leaders and senior managers are, by definition, responsible for the strategic direction of the business (often reviewed and initiated with board support and agreement). However, across a whole range of areas and responsibilities, the widest possible inclusion and engagement in the thinking and decision-making by middle managers and those on the ground responsible for actually 'doing' the task itself, cannot be underestimated.

In an environment and business culture in which everyone has an input into their role, functional, operational procedures and processes can, in the main, only result in one thing – improvement in efficiency and productivity.

Of course, there will always be those who turn up, do their job and go home, with no further thought as to whether the work they are doing is worthwhile. There will be those who don't want to assist in doing anything that requires additional input, thought or responsibility. For a large majority of people though, having an input and being allowed to think and innovate about their own role is hugely engaging, empowering and rewarding, not to mention beneficial for the organisation.

Enlisting the collective brains of five people doing a particular task is far more likely to result in progress towards enhanced capability, rather than relying solely on the brain of one manager alone.

The structures around which these things can develop will be specific to each business and sector, but, fundamentally, if time is taken to create the cultural environment and is then supported by the practical processes by which such a proposition can be activated, the generation of 'haste of solution' from your team, to whatever might be thrown up, will be greatly enhanced, already in place and entirely natural to them.

However well the inclusiveness of your cultural environment might function, unless haste is at the heart of any decisions subsequently, and however made, failure is a greater risk. So many businesses realise what needs to be done, know the personnel changes that need to be made, accept that processes or structures need radical overhaul and yet, they procrastinate.

Dithering in business, particularly around the difficult and more challenging areas of an operation, is a far more common problem amongst managers than may be thought.

The number of times we have heard managers and leaders say that they wish they had taken a decision earlier would be too great to list here.

One of the single most critical approaches to effective decision-making is, quite simply, this: once a decision has been made, GET ON WITH IT!

A 'no normal' leader always has an eye on the complications that too much bureaucracy brings to the organisation – tough on bureaucracy and tough on the causes of bureaucracy. Do not let the complication of processes get in the way of delivering your service.

Making wiser decisions should be an expectation built into the fabric of the culture and expectations of the business. Sensible weighing up of the pros and cons, including different viewpoints and perspectives and creating the best cultural environment to ensure that all of these elements are at their maximum, all contribute towards the making of sensible decisions.

'No normal' leaders not only facilitate such a process, they also strive to avoid 'group-think' and 'excuse-think' and openly value brainstorming as a way of inclusively engaging everyone who should have a voice, to have one.

Were we to have spent hours considering every point in this book in a particularly academic way, we might have come up with a formula for 'getting on with it'. But as we haven't we'll simply suggest six words and a + and = sign.

Wise Choice + Velocity = High Impact Outcome

The same singular focus of attention, particularly amongst the senior leadership team, can be necessary when delivering unity of purpose. It is totally unacceptable for managers to play their own personally ambitious games at the expense of the greater good.

Whatever the disagreements might be behind closed doors when tricky and challenging decisions have to be made, once a decision has been reached, everyone needs to get behind it.

Particularly at the senior level, the necessary openness of

deliberation and debate within a leadership team in private, once concluded, must give way to unity of message and purpose, in public.

6: Make Decisions Wisely

No normal leaders understand...

- An abundance of bureaucracy can be extremely frustrating. Tough on bureaucracy and its causes
- Significance of key systems and processes in forming plans
- Value of weighing up the pros, cons, benefits and consequences
- Value of different viewpoints and perspectives
- Importance of creating the very best environment for decisionmaking.

Even better when they grasp…

- Visualising impact of any decision can help to bring it home
- Risk of group and 'excuse-think'
- Need to facilitate thinking focused on clear goals for meetings, raising awareness, generating options and appropriate plans
- Value of brainstorming and reverse brainstorming
- Importance of investing sufficient time evaluating plans before taking action.

CHAPTER 12

Tentacle 7 – Communicate Openly and Clearly

"Ah, we do that already," we hear you say.

Well, unless you are one of a small number of businesses that actually do – we doubt it. We have one simple point to make in respect to communication.

BE OPEN & CLEAR
BE OPEN & CLEAR
BE OPEN & CLEAR

REPEAT
REPEAT
REPEAT

How you do this, we are not going to prescribe – e-mails, WhatsApp groups, noticeboards, online and real-time team meetings, internal digital mechanics, etc, etc. The list of options is substantial. It may be that one, or even all of these options, is appropriate.

Whatever processes you might opt for, openness, clarity and repetition are key. Not everyone in your organisation is as interested in what is going on as you are. Many will have forgotten what you tell them shortly after you've told them! Some will never read an e-mail from you and others genuinely think they are just passing through and couldn't care less.

But, for most, the majority of whom will be interested to one degree or another, the openness with which you communicate and the clarity with which you do it, will pay dividends in understanding later down the tracks.

Sharing information with your team is sometimes brave but almost always beneficial. If your team understands some of the challenges being faced, they will often take a more measured and responsible approach to conversations in and around the business. Additionally, assuming the cultural environment that facilitates it, they'll also be keener to suggest alternatives or ways to improve things.

Surely you want that level of engagement, particularly when the going is tough, or the latest crisis hits?

There are too many managers and leaders in the country who still believe that they are playing some kind of game of poker with their teams. It involves bluff and stake-raising and the final outcome is intended to 'take-all'.

Unfortunately for a small minority of bosses, though, it's all too often about taking rather than sharing; taking the credit rather than giving; greed rather than inclusiveness and generosity, and selfishness, rather than selflessness.

Well, we live in the 21st century and as people seek different and ever more lifestyle-focused ways of working, the managers and leaders who facilitate more meaningful engagement with their teams will be the ones who prosper and attract the best people to their organisations.

Open, clear and authentic communication is built upon Tentacle 1 – trust. If you get up and spout forth about almost any subject you can think of, but your team sit there and think to themselves, *Yeah, right, here we go again. He said that last time and it was all bollocks*, you'll sink without trace.

A 'no normal' leader is visible, accessible and interacts with the team at every opportunity. They clearly and succinctly promote the vision the company has with repetitive regularity. As well as the aspiration for their teams and the success they desire for the organisation itself, the 'no normal' business leader promotes the company's culture and brings their words to life with clearly identifiable actions, which support all that is being advocated.

One additional component of the 'no normal' approach regarding communication, which rarely receives its rightful share of the action, is listening. Communication at its best is a two-way process. A 'no normal' leader is one who recognises that (s)he must listen as well as speak and signal throughout the organisation that their ears are 'open for business'.

Finally, as will have become clear as your journey through this book continues, it is not any one of these things that creates the capability of the 'no normal-ready' business, but all of them together, overlapping and collectively deployed.

7: Communicate Openly and Clearly

No normal leaders understand...

- Open and clear communication is a core part of effective leadership
- It's not possible to communicate everything themselves
- Listening is vital and signals desire to work collaboratively
- Transparency is critical particularly when going through tough times
- Negativity can be extremely destructive.

Even better when they grasp…

- Leaders must be visible, accessible and ensure information is exchanged both ways
- Need for opportunity to interact, making the frequency, quality and impact of everyday conversations a cultural asset
- Value of collaborating on vision, values and strategy
- Importance of consistency in communication and key messaging. Bringing words to life with actions
- Revealing weaknesses and vulnerabilities in the spirit of openness can encourage the same openness in return.

CHAPTER 13

Tentacle 8 – Value Similarity and Difference

What an extraordinary world we live in and what a truly remarkable species the human being is – so many different colours, characteristics, qualities and appearances. A world of billions of individual entities, all of which should have so much in common and yet can so cruelly raise their potential for wrongdoing and inflict it to the disadvantage of their fellow man.

There is so much diversity and innate capacity to create and innovate as well as loyalty, love, compassion and a range of intellectual, as well as practical gifts possessed by people, that its breadth of potential achievement knows no bounds.

Just imagine, for a moment, what kind of world we could live in where all of those things were encouraged, developed and integrated into one enormous family business, whose objectives were change for good and enhancement of life.

It's a huge leap of philosophical and idealistic faith, but we want you to consider this approach in microcosm.

In any business, there will not only be a diverse range of mental and physical skills, qualities, characteristics and talents but often, there'll be equally as wide a range of physical characteristics – gender, sexual orientation, ethnicity and so on.

Allowing people to be themselves at work, relaxed, comfortable and supported in their own skin, as well as recognised for their own worth, is hugely empowering for them.

In a 'no normal' cultural environment, no-one should feel excluded and everyone should be encouraged to contribute in their own distinctive way.

Creating an environment in which those who toil for the business, do so with the open support and encouragement of others, but equally importantly, with the confidence and 'wraparound' personal and professional support and encouragement of their company – their commercial family – is altogether more powerful.

But, in addition to the physical and the mental accommodation that your business or organisation needs to make, the second vital factor to be widely openly encouraged and accepted is diversity of thought.

One of the amazing things about human beings is their extraordinary capacity to think differently, to look at the same thing and yet perceive it differently, to look at a problem or challenge and come up with a myriad of different ways in which a solution might be found – rather like 'thinking outside the box'. How incredible, how amazing and how fantastically lucky it is for the business that engages those diverse thoughts, views and opinions to the benefit of itself.

A business that captures a sense of belonging, of universal learning and development, that celebrates difference and similarity and delivers all of these things using inclusive language at every level, is definitely ready for their 'no normal' journey.

The embracing of diversity, in its widest sense, is the golden thread which could so readily tie together much of the cultural and practical fabric of the operation and produce truly remarkable results.

To conclude then, promoting such a concept requires leaps of faith and trust. Whether you have the faith or the desire to trust and be trusted is, of course, for you to decide.

Harness difference. It can often be a game changer.

This finalises the interpretation of the eight tentacles of the octopus.

8: Value Similarity and Difference

No normal leaders understand...

- Everyone gets to contribute in their own distinctive and valid way
- Diverse experiences. Differences in race, gender and socioeconomic background make the team stronger
- No-one must feel excluded
- The value of building an inclusive culture
- The dangers of 'hire like me' syndrome.

Even better when they grasp...

- Need for awareness of and acting on unconscious bias at every level
- Impact of feeling a sense of belonging and its value to individual learning and development
- Teams function best when tension and friction are seen to be part of a learning process
- Celebrating both similarity and difference, frequently, ignites invention and creativity
- Need to develop inclusive approaches and language at every level.

CHAPTER 14

Why Bother?

So, now for the moment of truth.

It's fair to say that most people who read this book will do absolutely nothing. They'll put it down and probably never pick it up again. Some will consider it to have been an interesting read and others will attempt to debunk it and condemn it as yet another in the latest round of 'fad business books'.

That's all cool with us; at least we actually did something and wrote it!

Amongst those who have got this far, however, will be a small minority of people who might just think it's worth bothering, worth taking a cold, hard look at their business and believe that it can be better.

If you are one of those, thank you for thinking. We say 'thinking' because any philosophical change such as this starts with that – thinking.

If you think that there are areas of operation that your business will benefit from in terms of review and action, the next step is so much easier to take.

If you think that just one enhancement, in just one area, will make a difference, your journey can begin.

If you think that you need your business to be 'no normal'-ready and that the strategies outlined in this book are what needs to happen to achieve that – happy days.

But, whatever your thoughts might be about the pages of this book as you worked your way through it, one thing, we hope, has been stirred in terms of your thinking.

Not bothering to do anything to prepare your business for what will certainly come in the future is not an option. 'No normal' normality is a fact of life. Fads come and go, but readiness, in its widest sense, is key and the capability to manage when it does, essential.

We wrote this book because we are business enthusiasts. We are fully signed-up members of the pro-business club. With all its faults, the commercial world is a powerful source for good and can be even better if it really chooses to be so.

We reject the 'new normal' arguments because we believe that they facilitate sloppy thinking when it comes to business and encourage 'excuse-think'. To conclude:

'No normal' is a state of readiness.

'No normal' is a simple but effective commercial skeleton around which the flesh of attitude, behaviour and practice can be wrapped.

'No normal' requires an acceptance that every challenge may be specifically new but all challenges have to be addressed and responded to in the appropriate way by businesses 'ready' when they happen for just those moments of angst and crisis.

'No normal' is normality and the better placed your organisation is to manage the inevitability of whatever 'new' comes its way, the better placed it will be to grow, prosper and thrive in what is an ever-changing business climate.

Whether you decide to bother or not is a matter for you. But think about this: people are remembered for what they do and not for what they meant to do.

How will you be remembered?

SELF-ASSESSMENT

How 'No Normal-ready' am I?

Below we have listed 27 statements which we believe will establish your degree of readiness in the 'no normal' world. We'd like you to read each one, think carefully and honestly about your score out of ten for each (10 being perfect and 1 being a disaster!) and then add up the total to grade yourself.

	LEADERS IN A 'NO NORMAL' WORLD	*Score*
1	I view today's 'no normal' world as business as usual and believe that 'no normal' survival requires an underlying state of readiness for any organisation and all its people	
2	I am ready to dynamically rethink, re-assess and re-invent my cultural, organisational and strategic approach to everything I do with everyone else	
3	I work on the readiness of my people to assimilate and respond with ever- greater velocity and capability	
4	I am clear about role-model attitudes, behaviours and habits required to thrive in a 'no normal' world	

5	I will go on to develop 'no normal' attitudes, behaviours and capabilities with my people via deliberate practice and preparation	
6	I will question yesterday's logic and ideas of reaching (the false premise of) a 'new normal' safety point, particularly in turbulent times	
7	I recognise that human beings like going back to (the often-idealised state of) normal	
8	I see my goal as reaching readiness, achieved by capability, embedded in a 'no normal' culture	
9	I avoid the *normal* traps of defensive and restrictive 'excuse-think' at all costs	
10	I am suspicious of phrases like 'Let's get back to normal' or 'We've reached a 'new normal' and am ready to challenge them	
11	I advocate 'no normal readiness' to deal with the effects of change, uncertainty and potentially catastrophic threats to my organisation	
12	I only recruit people with a growth mindset accompanied by a fierce willingness to learn	
13	I view running the whole show on my own as a serious readiness risk and a betrayal of the growth prospects of the business and its people	
14	I constructively challenge the status quo and am ready to be challenged back	
15	I fully license teams to challenge and encourage adaptation and creativity	

16	I facilitate continuous review/thinking and drive change as a result	
17	I focus on outcomes and the possibility of different futures	
18	I am often a catalyst for well-managed conflict and hissy fits over 'artistic differences'	
19	I prepare to be ready by considering intuitively and acting decisively	
20	I am an open and clear communicator, always ready to transmit and receive critical messages	
21	I never forget the value of regular, high-quality and effective conversation	
22	I trust my people and give them freedom to engage and flourish	
23	I ignite learning, performance and development opportunities	
24	I actively support and challenge performance and behaviour	
25	I have a healthy obsession with maximising roles, outcomes, timescales and results	
26	I make decisions wisely by enlisting collective brainpower and expertise	
27	I know how to harness similarity and difference to produce remarkable results	

IF YOU SCORED LESS THAN 135:

This is definitely not for you unless you're committed to quite some transformation.

IF YOU SCORED BETWEEN 135 AND 162:

It's a journey you can travel and you'll need to work hard on your mindset, but take the first few steps and begin the change.

IF YOU SCORED BETWEEN 162 AND 189:

You are already well on the way and you have all the attributes to making a seriously good first go at being a 'no normal' leader. Re-visit your scores once again in six months after setting yourself objectives to improve those aspects of your scorecard which fell below a score of 7.

IF YOU SCORED BETWEEN 189 AND 216:

You get it and, in the main, you're doing it. Re-visit those chapters in the book that target the small number of areas you recognise you're falling just a tad short in and then set yourself clear goals and objectives to address those areas. For you, it's all about marginal gains.

IF YOU SCORED OVER 216:

We should have consulted you when we wrote this book! Each chapter should be used to help you remain focused, remind you of your qualities and the rightness of your approach and to refresh your already strong leadership characteristics. You already get it and, what's more, you're doing it.

IF YOU SCORED 270:

Congratulations – you should have written the book instead of reading it!

WILLIAM ROGERS

The Sunday Times' Top 100 'Best Leader' of a mid-sized company for three years in a row (2012, 2013 and 2014), William Rogers is a 'people focused' manager, leader, entrepreneur and businessman.

Founder of an insurance broking business at the age of 24, William built the business from scratch until it was sold 28 years later in 2012.

In 2002, William became Chief Executive Officer of UKRD Group, a commercial radio group, which also co-owned a national advertising sales house and software development company, as well as holding interests in various broadcast transmission facilities.

UKRD Group was accredited as being the Number 1 Sunday Times' Top 100 'Best Mid-sized Company to Work For' in 2011, 2012, 2013 and 2014; a rare four times in a row.

William turned UKRD Group around from a loss-making company to one of consistent operating profitability. In 2009, he led a 'hostile' takeover bid for public company, The Local Radio Company, delivering one of the rarest successes achieved in such circumstances; when UKRD's bid defeated that of the alternative bidder, even though UKRD's cash offer was lower.

UKRD Group was sold to German media group, Bauer, in March 2019.

William has a particular passion for building strong company cultures, believing that people are the most important asset any business or organisation has and that they should be the central focus around which operational policies should be shaped and developed.

Outside of his professional life, William has been the chairman of a small housing society, chairman of a college of further education, primary school governor, elected councillor and leader of the local authority on which he served and was awarded the MBE in 1990 at the age of 30.

JONATHAN BRADLEY

Jonathan Bradley is a game-changing leader, executive coach and practitioner of organisational development. Coming from a corporate background in broadcast media, he established his company, Trimodus, in 2005 to transform the performance of leaders and teams.

Jonathan has implemented such programmes across wide-ranging industry sectors and organisations, including the University of Oxford, the British Horseracing Authority, Discovery Channel, TMF Group, IHS Markit Ltd, Cambridge University Press and Balfour Beatty.

Ever aware that "the future ain't what it used to be," he prepares organisations to be ready for change and to capitalise on uncertainty. His global leadership work has taken him across Asia, the Americas and Europe, while his on-line expertise includes webinars, mentoring, facilitation and podcasts.

Jonathan co-hosts a Global Leadership Podcast, challenging the status quo, asking the big questions and delivering fresh insights and solutions to performance-related problems. "There's no 'going back to normal,'" he says. "Instead, learn to thrive in a no-normal world."

DAVE COULL

Dave Coull's career began at the age of 16 when he joined his local radio station, FM107 The Falcon. At the time, the radio station was owned by UKRD Group; the company he would work at for the next 20 years and, during which, both his role and responsibilities would grow from that of 'work experience lad' to senior executive within the company.

At UKRD, as Group Content Director, he was primarily responsible for all the content delivered to market, on both traditional and digital platforms, and also, as a member of the company's senior executive team, for the transformational change of the business from that of traditional radio group, to successful multi-platform, multimedia company.

Dave launched and led 'Local Radio Day', an annual, industry-wide initiative that celebrated local radio across Local BBC, commercial, community and charitable radio stations, which also won 'Team of the Year' at the national audio and radio industry awards, the ARIAs.

He is a 'people focused' leader and has a particular interest in developing company cultures that work for all the stakeholders involved. Dave combines smart strategic thinking with the necessary commitment and detailed focus to deliver on the most ambitious of objectives.

Outside of his professional career, Dave loves nothing more than putting on his trainers and getting outside for a run.

Printed in Great Britain
by Amazon

59413763R00047